The Mercury Retrograde Book

Thriving

~~Surviving~~ During Mercury Retrograde

The Mercury Retrograde Book

Thriving
~~Surviving~~ During Mercury Retrograde

Therese Francis, Ph.D.

Crossquarter Breeze
PO Box 8756
Santa Fe, NM 87504-8756

First printing 2000
ISBN: 1-890109-33-9

Printed in the United States of America on recycled paper.

Publisher's Cataloging-in-Publication

(Provided by Quality Books, Inc.)

Francis, Therese
The Mercury retrograde book: thriving during Mercury retrograde / Therese Francis -- 1st ed.
p. cm.
LCCN: 00-190668
ISBN: 1-890109-33-9

1. Astrology. 2. Mercury (Planet) I. Title

BF1724.2.M45F73 2000 133.5'33
QBI00-492

Contents

Appendices

Acknowledgements

Thanks to Dante Ruiz, Estelle Daniels, Judith Hamlin, Paul Tuitean, Peter Smith, Heather Rowntree, and Julia Deisler for their contributions to this book. Without your contributions, this book would not exist.

Introduction

It's 5:43 p.m. July 12, 1999 in Santa Fe, New Mexico. Mercury was at exact station less than 10 minutes ago. It is now "retrograde" (more on what that means later). I've spent all day getting everything done that needed to be finished before Mercury stationed and entered its approximately 21-day retrograde interval.

I've been looking forward to this Mercury retrograde interval for two weeks now. I haven't always been so enthused about retrograde Mercury. Like many people, I, too, have rolled my eyes at the announcement that Mercury is now retrograde and that's why... (fill in the blank with the car won't start, the computer crashed, the parcel is lost in the mail, the check won't clear the bank, the contract needs to be renegotiated, and so on).

Why is that important? Because I've learned to live (or at least make an effort to live) my life in synch with the cosmic cycles, especially those of the planet Mercury. One of my teachers constantly reminds me that the better part of valor is preservation. And that's the reason I have started following Mercury's cycles. I've been beaten with the proverbial 2x4 too many times to continue ignoring Mercury's cycles. And I've watched too many other people get "beaten up" during these intervals.

Actually, I've watched enough disasters, counseled enough people through heartaches, and needed to repair enough damaged communication lines that have occurred during Mercury retrograde intervals to start asking, "Is there anything good about these intervals?"

I'm happy to report—Yes.

Do Planets Really Move Backwards?

No, planets don't really move backwards, but from the Earth they occasionally look like they do. The process of appearing to move forward, stop, move backwards, stop and then move forward again is called a retrograde cycle (see the figure on page 2).

Direct

When a planet appears to be moving forward, it is referred to as direct.

Stationing

Just before Mercury switches to being retrograde or direct, it appears to stand still.[1]

---

[1] Appendix A provides a table of stationing times and positions for Mercury. Appendix B contains instructions for determining exact local time of station.

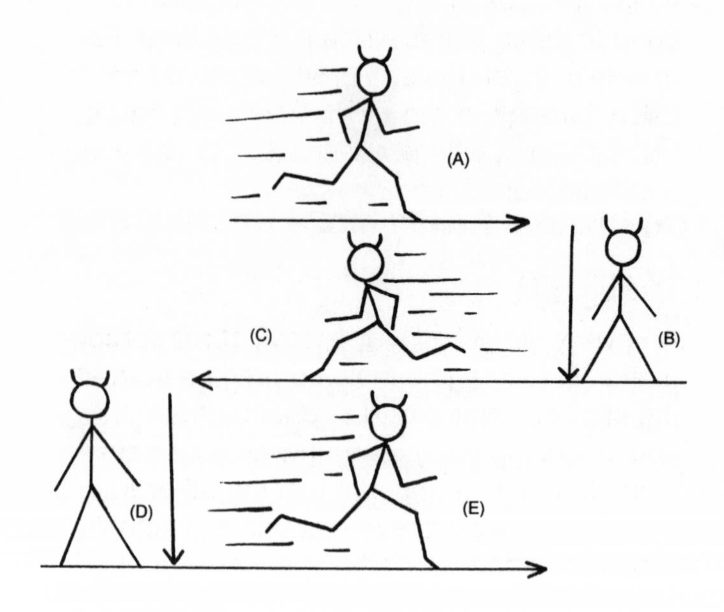

A planet appears to move forward (A), stand still (B), move backward (C), stand still (D), and move forward again. This is called the retrograde cycle. Mercury is said to be in its shadow while it appears to retrace its path for the third time (E).

This time period is referred to as stationing (the two figures that are standing still). It is abbreviated either as SR (changing from direct to retrograde) or as SD (changing from retrograde to direct).

Stationing times are very powerful. The consequences of anything started, said, or done at these points will last a long time. For example, if you make a promise you'd best follow through or the ramifications will haunt you for years, whether it is just a "I'll call you in 5 minutes" or a wedding vow.

Retrograde

An overly simplified way to look at retrograde motion is to imagine that you are in a train at the station, parked next to another train. If you're looking out the window as your train starts to move, it appears that the other train is moving backwards, even though it is actually staying still and your train is the one moving.

Now, if you ask an astronomer to explain retrograde motion, you'll get a very scientific discourse on angle of motion against the sun, *et cetera*. My encyclopedia has 5-1/2 pages of small print explaining retrograde motion and the different phases of such. All you really need to know is that the planet *appears* to be moving backward but is actually moving forward; it's a cosmic optical illusion.

All of our solar system's planets have retrograde intervals. Mercury retrogrades about three times a year for approximately three weeks each time. Venus retrogrades the least, about every 1-1/2 years for 6 weeks, and Pluto has the longest retrograde intervals, up to 23 weeks.

Astrologically, a retrograde time (regardless of the planet) is interpreted as a turning of the energy of the planet inward instead of outward.

Shadow

A planet is bobbing along, doing its thing; then it stations, turns around, and goes retrograde for a bit, stations, and then returns to direct motion. The initial part of its path after returning to direct motion is a retracing of its original path. The overlap time is called the shadow.

Introducing Mercury

Heeerrre's Mercury

The planet Mercury is named for the Roman messenger god, Mercury (called Hermes in the Greek pantheon). Mercury is pictured with winged shoes or wings on his heels that enable him to fly on errands at the speed of the wind (in ancient times believed to be the speed of thought). On a normal day, watching Mercury flying between locations delivering messages, insights, travelers, and commands could get you dizzy.

In astrology, his realm includes communication (especially oral), messages, transportation, and the intellectual mind. He is the negotiator between the conscious and subconscious mind, and he shares the dream world with Neptune. Mercury also represents curiosity, the thirst for knowledge, ambition, and the ability to learn.

When the planet Mercury goes retrograde, it's as though the god Mercury finally sits down for a breather. He uses this time to plan out the next barrage of flights. You should do the same.

What Not To Do

Since most astrology books spend a few paragraphs telling you what not to do during a retrograde period, I'll start in the same place. Then we can use the remainder of this book to address what *to* do.

Mercury rules communications. Everything in everyday life involves communications. When the god of communications sits down for a break, expect communications to come to a standstill. This will affect every form of communication—from satellites to intra-family messages to transportation.

The results can range from frustrating to aggravating to dangerous.

Some common examples are the mail taking longer to get to its destination (or maybe you forgot to put a stamp on the envelope), storms interfering with satellite transmissions, one (important) page of the business plan getting missed by the photocopier, the replacement mother board on your computer not working (and neither does its replacement), and the dress that looked terrific in the store turning out to be the wrong shade to match the shoes.

During these three-week periods judgments and decision-making are likely to be wrong (generally due to inaccurate, incomplete, or unavailable details). Anything started during this time is likely to need to be redone.

Transportation mess-ups will be common, including plane schedules being off.

Be cautious of directions received during a Mercury retrograde interval: something important might be left out, there might be an unexpected detour, or the numbers will be transposed. Even if the directions are correct, your vehicle might develop an unexplainable technical problem.

The rule is this: while Mercury is retrograde don't start anything new, make important decisions, buy anything (especially appliances, which are ruled by Mercury), or take actions that you want to have lasting effects.

What's a Mercury retrograde book without some horror stories? Let's look at some examples of what can happen during a retrograde Mercury interval.

Fixing the Computer

Recently my friend's friend, we'll call her Jill, had a mother board "blow" on a client's computer on the first day of a retrograde Mercury. She ordered a replacement through a company that guarantees overnight delivery. Something happened and the board did not arrive.

Several days later she ordered another board.

The first board finally arrived, on the same day as the second board. Unfortunately, neither one worked.

So the client decided to buy a new computer. During most of the year, the new computer would have taken three days to arrive.

Two weeks later, the computer arrived—on the day that Mercury went direct.

How Bad Can It Get?

Here's an example of how much chaos can occur in just three weeks (actually, this is the abridged version). Fortunately, most people do not experience this much disorder in a lifetime of Mercury retrogrades as this fellow did in one. Here's his story:

About four years ago, my wife and I were living in Bayville, Long Island. We experienced the most intense period of Mercury retrograde incidents to happen to us before or since.

On the first day of Mercury retrograde both of us experienced multiple equipment failures in our respective workplaces: photocopiers, phones, computers, and even a normally reliable coffee machine—all refused to work properly.

I was working in Manhattan and depended on the train to commute to and from work. Upon arriving at Penn Station that evening, I discovered the railway workers would be starting a strike the next day, which would suspend rail services for who knew how long.

When I got home I realized that I should have gone to a friend's house four miles away. My wife had not been clear about which night we were expected there for dinner.

The next day I managed to get into Manhattan by train, but the train was one hour late.

I, and several colleagues, found ourselves locked out of our workplace because the usually dependable front desk person had fallen ill and stayed home, unwittingly holding on to the keys for the front door. Someone had to catch a bus to her home to retrieve the keys. So, in effect, I was about 100 minutes late for work.

Both phones and computers were malfunctioning all day causing massive frustration for me and my co-workers. Incoming callers frequently found themselves cut off in mid-conversation.

A usually friendly and placid customer came in and erupted with rage because her reservation for a seminar had been lost and the seminar was now totally full. (Over the next few days there was a succession of similar incidents as one "cock up" after another was uncovered.)

My wife experienced a major security breach at the Battered Wives' Shelter where she worked. The whereabouts of the Shelter was supposed to be kept secret—for obvious reasons—and one of the "inmates" confessed that she had told her abusing boyfriend the location. This necessitated a whole slew of phone calls (to police, Social Services, etc.) and an emergency meeting of the Shelter staff. Eventually it came out that she had unwittingly told him the wrong street!

When I finished work and got to Penn Station, there was a partial stoppage of train services and part of my journey home was by bus. The bus driver didn't know the way and we almost got lost. I ended up directing him the last five miles!

On the way home from her work, my wife's car started to malfunction and she only just made it back.

When she got home, she pressed the "Play" button on our answering machine and got three messages in what sounded like Arabic (no kidding!). We don't know anyone who speaks Arabic, nor do we understand it!

Next morning there was a high wind. About 10 a.m., whilst both of us were at work or on the way (my train was again one hour late arriving), the telephone pole at the top of our driveway fell over, putting a deep dent in the trunk of my wife's car, which was parked in the driveway awaiting attention for its aforementioned malfunction.

The pole brought down the telephone line so I couldn't get through at the end of the day to tell my wife that the train stoppage was total and I was staying over in Manhattan that night. I spent a half hour talking to our phone company who I thought was at fault and had disconnected us because of some mix up over our bill (which WAS late in being paid that month, but I had sent the check the day before Mercury went retrograde).

Next day, a fax I had sent to Amsterdam that morning was returned—from a number in Greece!

One of my colleagues programmed the main photocopier to make 100 copies of a flyer and then left. When she returned an hour later it had emptied its entire magazine of paper and we had about 700 copies, none of which were any good because the machine had "disobeyed" the instruction to print both sides of the flyer—well, not exactly, it had printed the same side of the original on both sides of every sheet!

When the phone company came to put up a new pole, the work truck backed into a fire hydrant nearby. We had a veritable flood of water! While this was being attended to by the water company, the phone company successfully erected another pole but messed up the cable connection to our house, so we STILL didn't have a phone. It took another two days before they returned and fixed the fault.

After work I had arranged for a colleague to take me to Jamaica, NY, where I could get a train connection home. She was out on assignment in the City and forgot all about me. I had to spend another night sleeping in the Massage Room at the Center.

Mercifully that was it. There were no further incidents of a major nature, though the phones, computers, and trains continued to be unreliable for the next three weeks until Mercury went direct!

I'm sure you have your own "horror" stories or have heard ones from friends and family. Is it any wonder why brave people start to quiver when they find out that Mercury is soon to be retrograde?

Change Your Perceptions, Change Your World

Mercury Perceived as Enemy

Stories like these have led to the common perception of Mercury retrograde as the "enemy" of sane, orderly life. Many people have adopted the roll-the-eyes-and-moan response upon hearing that Mercury is about to go retrograde. Even you might occasionally feel that the Universe must be out to get you. Many a brave soul has quivered at the news of an upcoming retrograde.

And for good reason.

Normally the god Mercury is looking at the external world. But when Mercury is retrograde, it's as though he's looking at the

When Mercury is retrograde, you may feel that the Universe is staring at you.

internal world—you. Most people are not comfortable with that level of attention.

Mercury Perceived as Teacher

But this does not need to be a dreaded encounter every three months. Contrary to the attitude of many astrology books on the market, Mercury retrograde is a great time. There are many things that can be successfully accomplished during these three-week intervals. And, if you start working in harmony with the retrograde cycle, you will benefit greatly.

The first step in developing a congenial relationship with Mercury is to allow Mercury to be your teacher. Mercury rules the third house in astrology, the house of early education. Mercury teaches us the basics about how life works. He teaches us be in harmony with Universal cycles.

When a person is deprived of sleep for more than 72 hours, he or she starts to exhibit psychotic behavior. Sleep is a necessary part of life.

Just as we need to sleep in regular intervals for optimal performance, we all need down time from our active lives, time to plan, dream, think, evaluate, rest, and regroup. Then we can "wake up" to optimal efficiency and effectiveness. Why just run the rat race when you can be in control of how difficult the terrain is? Smooth out the curves by resting when the Universe provides a rest period.

If we take time out, we can see these cycles and gather energy from them.

Then we can approach the retrograde cycle as a friend.

Mercury Perceived as Friend

Mercury can be your friend. Not just any friend, but the best kind: one that is predictable and reliable. The Mercury retrograde cycle occurs about every three months. That's three to four times each year—very predictable.

You can see it coming, so use it.

Several years ago, I heard about a small business owner, let's call her Joanne, who decided Mercury could be her friend.

Using Mercury to Improve a Business

> Joanne owns a small advertising firm. Advertising firms work on tight deadlines. People who work in the advertising field are on constant overload, overtime, and high stress. Employee turnover is high, and burnout happens, even to the best, within a few years.
>
> Joanne, after learning about the Mercury retrograde cycle, decided to keep track of projects in relation to the Mercury cycle. Was a project done on time? Within budget? Were there many changes after the project got started? Was the client satisfied? She found that projects taken on during Mercury retrograde periods never happened under budget, seldom got done on time, and almost always had some important aspect of the project left out of the initial discussion (meaning lots of backtracking).
>
> She decided, against the advice of many peers and some of her employees, not to accept jobs when Mercury was retrograde. Instead, the

company would use the time to clean up work spaces, finish outstanding projects, reorganize supply closets, catch up on filing and invoicing, network, discuss any needs for restructuring or change, and settle internal problems.

Contrary to the naysayers, business actually improved. Projects taken on (when Mercury was direct) were, more often than not, finished before deadlines and under budget. Most clients have adjusted to the new arrangements (some clients who moved their jobs to other companies have since brought their business back after seeing the results). Employees feel less stressed, despite an increased workload. Overtime has decreased. Job satisfaction has increased. Turnover and burnout are now the exception rather than the rule.

This story can be yours, if you choose to perceive Mercury as your friend.

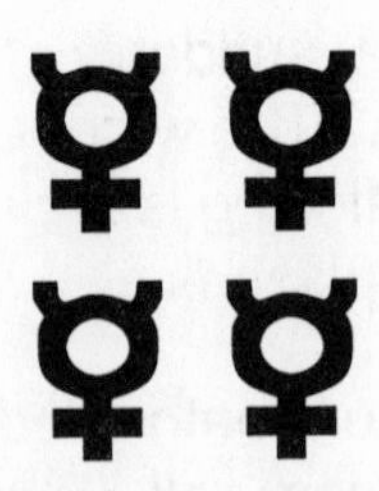

To Everything There Is a Season

Think of the Mercury retrograde cycle as having four parts: breathe deep, get ready, get set, and go.

Breathe Deep: Mercury Stations

When Mercury stands still, you should too. The day before the station (regardless of whether Mercury is going retrograde or direct), the day of station, and the day after, don't make decisions, take actions, start anything, or say anything that you don't want to haunt you.

Now's the time that most extreme Mercury retrograde stories happen. Why? Think of stirring a large container of water. What happens when you suddenly start stirring the opposite direction? The water splashes all over. Mercury stationing is very similar—the Mercury energy splashes all over.

Take these days to breathe deep and be (figuratively speaking) still. "Don't stir the pot."

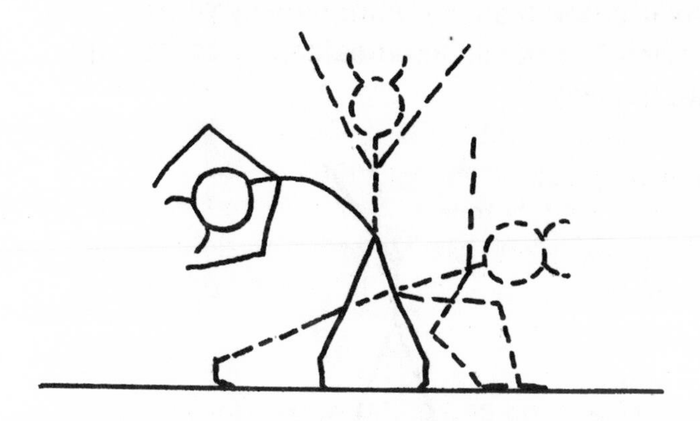

Get Ready: Mercury Retrograde

Think of Mercury retrograde as the get-ready phase. Don't plan on getting anything started during this time. If you get anxious to do something, think about whether you want to get it done right the first time. If so, wait. Put the energy into planning, investigating, gathering parts, sorting files, and resting.

Get Set: Mercury's Shadow

Think of Mercury's shadow as the get-set phase. Don't actually start yet, but get set to let yourself back into the race. Only now you're rested, with lots of energy and a clear vision of where you want to go. If you get anxious to get started, just remember that this, too, shall pass. Use this time to clean up messes that occurred during Mercury retrograde. Use the energy to be prepared. In the same way that Mercury retrograde is like a time out or the break between innings, Mercury's shadow is like stretching and doing warm-ups before jumping back into the game.

This is cosmic clean-up time. Any messes that occurred during the retrograde interval (because you didn't honor the retrograde and adjust your activities and expectations appropriately) now need to be put back on course. Also, any information that was not readily available during the retrograde comes to the surface.

For example, if you signed a contract to buy a house while Mercury was retrograde (generally not a good idea!), now you'll find out all the reasons why you should have waited: the electrical system is not up to code, there's an old city garbage dump under the garden in the back yard, you and the previous owner had a different definition of "major appliances included" (you were thinking refrigerator and he was thinking water heater), and the neighbor's son has a not-ready-for-prime-time rock band that practices every weekend in the family garage (next to your bedroom window).

Go: Mercury Direct

As soon as Mercury gets beyond its shadow, it's time to return to normal activity—the go phase. Use all the information you gathered during the retrograde phase to direct your actions. Use your renewed sense of self, your clear vision, and your rested body to accomplish far more than you could have without the down time.

Remember, the best athletes take breaks during the game because they know it optimizes their capabilities, and the best coaches call for time-outs to re-evaluate the game plan. Why would you want anything less in the game of life?

What to Do

So, you might ask, “What’s left to do during these three-week periods?” Lots. When any planet is retrograde, the energy is focused inward instead of outward to the world of manifestation. So during a retrograde Mercury, focus your mental energies inward instead of acting outward.

There are three types of activities that are great during retrograde Mercury: re’s, cleaning, and planning.

Just about any activity that starts with “re-” is a good retrograde activity:

- Re-create
- Rearrange
- Redo
- Reapply
- Reassemble
- Reevaluate

- Regress
- Remember
- Reorganize
- Restore
- Rethink
- Reunite
- Revise
- Relocate
- Renew
- Repair
- Restructure
- Retouch
- Review

This is also the time to do clean-up activities:

- Clean the closet or garage
- Rake leaves
- Follow up on projects
- Return phone calls

The exception to the "don't make decisions" during a retrograde rule is:

- Make decisions that you've been putting off (that are long overdue)

Mercury retrograde is also a great time for finding lost items and people. If you're looking for a classmate that you haven't seen in 20 years, start the search during a Mercury retrograde.

Finally, it's a good time to plan:

- Research
- Reflect
- Investigate
- Plan

This is a cosmic “lose a turn” space on the board of life, where you get to watch what’s going on around you and plan your next activity. It’s a good time to get above the daily swirl of activity and look at the big vision of how you want things to fit together.

Survival Tactics

In our modern fast-paced world (very Mercurial), we may not have the option of not doing the not-recommended activities. So here's some ideas for surviving when you don't have the option of not signing the contract, not traveling on a business trip, or not taking on new work.

Before Mercury Goes Retrograde

- Back up your computer files.
- Pay all the due bills, and any that will be due while Mercury is retrograde.
- Send birthday presents and letters.
- Buy clothes, shoes, or anything else that you might need while Mercury is retrograde.

- Make copies of directions and phone numbers for important appointments, travel itineraries, and emergency numbers. Place them in several locations (like near the phone, in your date book, and in your car).

While Mercury Is Retrograde

- Read the fine print.
- Ask questions. Then ask questions to clarify the answers.
- Use carry-on luggage.
- Bring a book so you have something to do when the meeting is delayed or the plane is late.
- Call for departure and arrival times before leaving for the airport.
- Confirm all appointments that morning. Leave a phone number where you can be reached in case a last minute change is needed. (Remember to check your messages frequently.)
- Bring a map. Look up alternate routes before you leave so you can avoid detours, traffic jams, and incorrect directions.
- Don't take anything for granted.
- Keep the sales slip.

While Mercury Is In Shadow

- Re-read any contracts that were signed during the previous three weeks for possible renegotiation.
- Ask those questions you forgot to ask.
- Begin to apply the research you've been doing these past three weeks (for example, about stocks to buy or sell).
- Clean up any and all miscommunications that occurred during the past three weeks.
- Check any equipment that "broke" during Mercury retrograde. You may find that it works fine now, or the answer is something simple that you are capable of doing (such as making sure the cord is completely plugged in).

Getting More Specific

At Home

You can tailor your activities based on which sign(s) Mercury occupies during a retrograde period. Appendix A lists dates and times of stations, along with the exact location. Let's use November 30 and December 20, 2004 as our first example.

The first column indicates which direction Mercury is changing to. In our example, on November 30, Mercury changes to "Retrograde" and on December 20 it returns to "Direct".

The next column is the date Mercury stations and changes direction. The third column is the time of station. (You can ignore these two columns for this chapter.)

The fourth column is the location in the zodiac at the time of station. In this example, on November 30, 2004, Mercury stations at 26 degrees 45 minutes Sagittarius. Mercury becomes direct again December 20, at 10 degrees 28 minutes Sagittarius. For this Mercury retrograde period, Mercury stays in Sagittarius. (For our purposes right now, you only need to know that Mercury is in Sagittarius; you can ignore the degrees and minutes until you are ready to start using aspects in chapter 6.)

Direction	Date	Time	Location
Retrograde	Nov 30 2004	12:10	26°Sg45'
Direct	Dec 20 2004	06:22	10°Sg28'

Table 1 lists the areas of influence for each of the 12 zodiac signs.

Table 1. Areas of Influence for Each Sign

Sign	Areas Affected
Aries	the body, beginning things, being at the cutting edge, assertiveness, aggression, wars and conflicts, x-games
Taurus	settling down, possessions, money, talents, culture, traditional knowledge, music
Gemini	learning, communicating, early education, reading, siblings, neighbors, the media, short trips

continued

Table 1. Areas of Influence for Each Sign (continued)

Sign	Areas Affected
Cancer	home, mother, nurturing, creativity
Leo	creativity, sports, games, war, gambling, arts, children, entertainment, the self
Virgo	service, daily habits, work, small animals, health, perfection, problem-solving, agriculture
Libra	family, relationships, partnerships, the arts, diplomacy
Scorpio	others' resources, banks, taxes, attorneys, legal issues, spying, mysteries, war, religion, metaphysics, sex, scandals
Sagittarius	philosophy, higher education, friendships, social clubs, organizations, college, travel, other countries/cultures, team sports, justice
Capricorn	work, duties, ethics, manifesting dreams, long-term planning
Aquarius	revolution, fanaticism, Truth, reform, humanitarian issues, needs of group vs. the individual, technology, philanthropy, electricity, society
Pisces	religion, spirituality, institutions (hospitals, jails, etc.), faith, alternative healing and education, dreams, visions, atomic research

So, between November 30 and December 20, 2004, when Mercury is in Sagittarius, you can tailor your activities to compensate for trouble in areas ruled by Sagittarius:

- Expect travel delays, especially those between countries
- Plan extra time into your travel arrangements (or, best, put off travel until Mercury returns to direct)
- Look for odd mix-ups in the judicial systems
- Verify dates and times for court hearings
- Plan extra time to get your new car registered

Let's try another example: November 14 to December 4, 2005. In this example, Mercury starts to retrograde in one sign and goes back into the previous sign (starts in Sagittarius and moves back into Scorpio).

Direction	Date	Time	Location
Retrograde	Nov 14 2005	05:36	10°Sg55'
Direct	Dec 4 2005	02:17	24°Sc46'

When tailoring your activities during this retrograde period, you need to take two signs into account—Sagittarius *and* Scorpio. Good things to do during these three weeks are:

- Being with friends (Sagittarius)
- Correcting an injustice from earlier times (Sagittarius)
- Reading mysteries (Scorpio)
- Reviewing your will (Scorpio)
- Writing in your journal (Scorpio).

Table 2 is a short list of ideas for you to do when Mercury is in each of the zodiac signs. This list is to get your idea-generator started; it is far from an exhaustive list.

Table 2. Some Ideas of What To Do During a Specific Retrograde Mercury

Sign	Things To Do
Aries	• Play games with your children (and let them win) • Investigate starting your own business • Start a martial art, like Tai Chi Ch'uan
Taurus	• Look at your financial situation • Invite friends to dinner • Go to a museum or concert (especially free ones) • Research retirement options • Talk with family members

continued

Table 2. Some Ideas of What To Do During a Specific Retrograde Mercury (continued)

Sign	Things To Do
Gemini	• Read all those books in your "to read" pile • Write letters of the "hi-how-are-you" type (especially to anyone you haven't contacted in a long time) • Call your siblings • Make follow-up calls you've put off
Cancer	• Clean the hallway closet • Iron out differences with your mother or re-connect • Take extra long baths (with the telephone turned off) • Take a cooking class
Leo	• Attend a high school drama presentation or band concert (especially if your child is in it) • Learn to use a computer (but don't purchase one) • Finish any outstanding craft projects (like the needlepoint piece you started three years ago) • Join a drama club • Plan a party

continued

Table 2. Some Ideas of What To Do During a Specific Retrograde Mercury (continued)

Sign	Things To Do
Virgo	• Research about the next family pet (but don't get a new pet until Mercury goes direct) • Give your internal editor a break—no self criticism for at least three minutes • Clean the garage • Picnic in the park with your co-workers • Write in your journal • Prepare the garden
Libra	• Try on all your clothes and give the ones that no longer fit to charity • Go to the museum • Take a painting class • Go to a poetry reading • Play a musical instrument • Rearrange furniture
Scorpio	• Do regression therapy to discover your past lives • Journal—get to those deep thoughts • Read a mystery or spy thriller • Review your will, living will, power of attorney, etc.

continued

Table 2. Some Ideas of What To Do During a Specific Retrograde Mercury (continued)

Sign	Things To Do
Sagittarius	• Party • Clean up the roadside or the river • Research justice • Research applying for graduate school • Plan your next voyage • Pull out the family photo album and reminisce (especially with your grandchildren)
Capricorn	• Investigate a new career or a career move you might like to make • Go on a retreat • Research future stock purchases • Reconnect with your father • Organize your work space • Work out how you might manifest a dream
Aquarius	• Rent videos • Research charities for philanthropic giving • Spend time volunteering at the local food shelter or assist at your church • Do research on the Internet • Take a tour of a movie set, radio station, or TV station

continued

Table 2. Some Ideas of What To Do During a Specific Retrograde Mercury (continued)

Sign	Things To Do
Pisces	• Dream—BIG • Do psychic development exercises • Read essays on world peace or biographies of great spiritual people • Splash in the ocean (a big puddle will do in a pinch)

In the News

The sign that Mercury occupies during a retrograde period (and its shadow) flavors life all over this planet. Expect a breakdown in communications (misunderstandings, withheld information, poor translations, and such) and travel snafus in the areas of influence for the sign occupied by Mercury (Table 1).

For example, if Mercury retrogrades in Leo, expect issues around self image, children, sports, games, and creativity to come under scrutiny. The government might start looking at child welfare laws. The arts will be in the news. A scandal might occur with a sports figure who acted impulsively (and irresponsibly).

A historical example is the atomic bombing of Japan. After the bombing of Hiroshima, Japan made an offer of peace. But the message was first delayed and then mistranslated, resulting in a second atomic bomb being dropped on Nagasaki. During this time, Mercury was retrograde in Leo (incidentally, Japan's ruling planet).

Transiting Houses

You'll need your birth chart (called your "natal chart") for this chapter.[1]

In Western astrology, your chart is done from the moment of your first breath. (Other systems, such as Chinese astrology, use the moment of conception.)

If you don't have the exact time of your first breath, you can have a "guess" chart done based on "somewhere around dinner time" or "near midnight." A "guess" chart, however, may not be accurate, so you'll need to keep track of how your actual experiences do or do not match up to your "guess" chart. Then you can

---

[1] See Appendix C if you have Mercury retrograde in your natal chart. Natal Mercury retrograde changes the experience of a transiting Mercury retrograde.

adjust your chart as needed to match your actual experiences. This may take years. Or you can have a professional astrologer do a rectification chart for you. (Your astrologer will ask you about important things that have happened in your life and then adjust the chart to match those events.)

If you don't have any idea of when you were born, use noon (12 p.m.) as the chart time. Follow your experiences as above, and adjust your chart.

Start with the Simple Stuff: Transiting Houses

When you feel comfortable with planning your activities based on where Mercury is located during a retrograde period, you're ready to add the next step: customizing your activities by looking at your own chart and comparing it to the current position of Mercury. Comparing the current location of a planet (such as Mercury) to your natal chart is called "transiting."

The simplest way to customize your activities during Mercury retrograde is to ignore the locations of the planets at your birth and look at the houses only. Where does a specific Mercury retrograde fit into your chart? (You won't be able to do this part if you don't have your actual time of birth, so skip to the next chapter.)

Table 3 lists key words associated with each of the houses. Choose your activities based on which house(s) are affected in your natal chart.

Table 3. Key Words for Each House

House	Areas Affected
1	physical body, how you appear in the world
2	personal resources, talents, money, possessions, jewelry
3	early learning, teaching, primary education, communications, short trips
4	home life, the home, real estate, mother (and mother issues)
5	creativity, children, sports, games, gambling, arts
6	service, daily habits, work, small animals, health
7	family, relationships, partnerships, contracts
8	other people's money and resources, secrets, taxes, the occult, sex, public enemies
9	higher education, distant travel, other cultures, in-laws, religions, philosophy
10	public image, career, reputation, father (or father issues), government
11	friends, social interactions, peers, income from profession, groups, organizations
12	institutions (hospitals, jails, etc.), secret enemies, hidden power, the unconscious, psychic gifts, spirituality

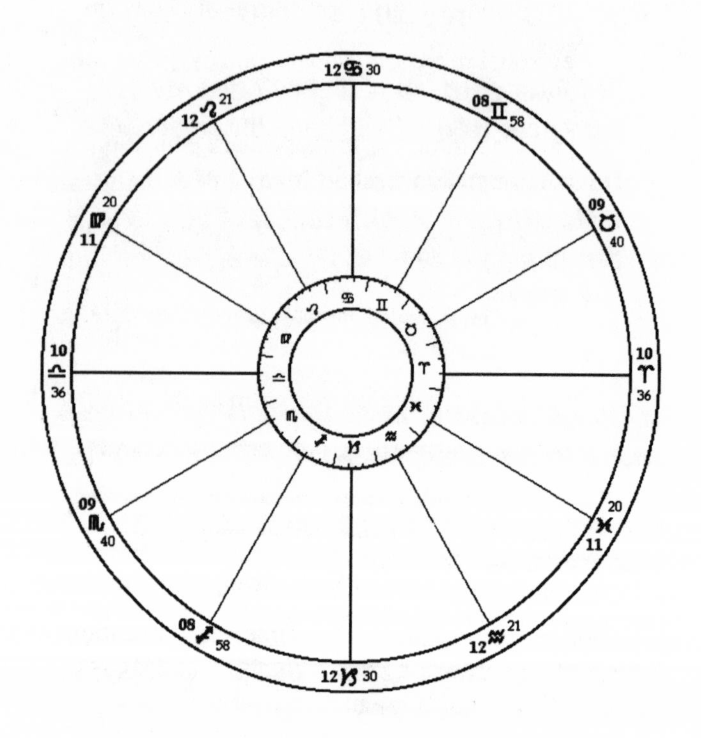

John's chart

Let's look at John's chart as an example. The retrograde interval from March 12 to April 4, 2012 starts at 6 degrees Aries and moves back to 23 degrees Pisces.

Direction	Date	Time	Location
Retrograde	Mar 12 2012	07:43	06°Ar49'
Direct	Apr 4 2012	10:05	23°Pi51'

In John's chart, all of the indicated Mercury retrograde interval will be in the sixth house.

He could use this time to learn a new language, write letters, or teach a colleague how to do a part of his job so he could take a vacation in a few weeks.

But what happens when Mercury retrogrades back into the previous sign?

The November 14 to December 4, 2005 retrograde period is an example.

Direction	Date	Time	Location
Retrograde	Nov 14 2005	05:36	10°Sg55'
Direct	Dec 4 2005	02:17	24°Sc46'

During this interval, Mercury will start in Mary's 10th house and moved back into her 9th house (10 degrees Sagittarius to 24 degrees Scorpio).

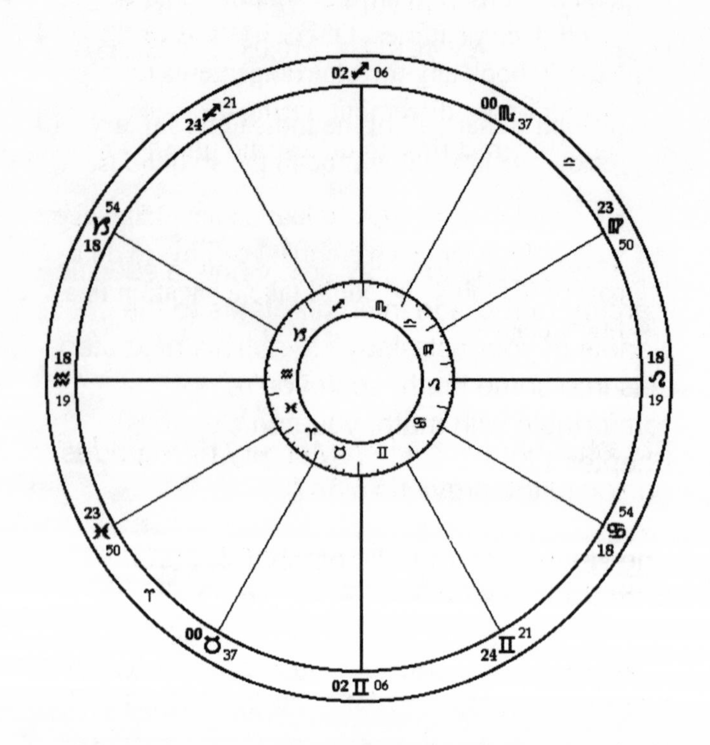

Mary's chart

This will be a good time for her to examine issues around career/public image and higher education/philosophy/far travel. Combining the energies of the 10th and 9th houses, these three weeks it will be good for her to dream about where she'd like to travel for work-related sales presentations, to read travel guides, and to watch documentaries. Of course, she won't actually book any travel arrangements until Mercury goes direct, but during the retrograde will be a great time to dream and plan.

The next step is to be aware of how a specific Mercury retrograde interval relates to the planets in your astrology chart. This next step gets into some math, so, if you're not comfortable with math, you can skip to Chapter 12.

Transiting Aspects

Once you've gotten the hang of transiting houses, you can look at transiting aspects (if you're brave and not afraid of the math).

This step involves comparing the positions of the planets at your birth to the current position of Mercury. Such interactions are called "aspects by transit." You can do transiting aspect for all the planets except the Moon if you don't have your time of birth.

(Yes, astrologers know that the Sun is not a planet, but for simplicity, the Sun, Moon, the planets, planetoids, asteroids, fixed stars, lunar nodes, etc., are collectively referred to as "planets.")

If you are doing your own mathematics, you'll have any easier time if you convert the positions to polar coordinates. See Appendix D for details.

The aspects that are most important are listed in the table below. Each of these aspects has a fancy name and a fancy symbol.

To make this slightly more complex, a planet that is within a specified number of degrees from being in one of the above aspects is considered to be in aspect. The specified number of degrees before or after the exact aspect is called the orb. What's confusing is that astrologers don't agree on how big the orb should be. Some like very small orbs, called "tight orbs," while others think that larger ones work. For simplicity, use the orbs listed in the chart. Just know that any given astrologer might argue with what's in the table.

Table 4. Major Aspects

Degrees Apart	Aspect Name	Symbol (Glyph*)	Orb
0	conjunct	☌	0-10 or 350-360 degrees
60	sextile	⚹	50-70 or 290-310 degrees
90	square	□	80-100 or 260-280 degrees
120	trine	△	110-130 or 230-250 degrees
180	opposite	☍	170-190 degrees

*See Appendix E for information on glyphs.

So, if your natal Jupiter is 55 degrees from the current Mercury, Mercury is sextiling Jupiter by transit. Look in the table and see that 55 degrees is in the orb of a sextile; it is between 50 and 70 degrees.

Likewise, if Jupiter is 305 degrees from the current Mercury, it is sextiling Jupiter by transit. Why? Because the 12 signs make a circle, and a circle is 360 degrees in a polar coordinate system. Therefore, 0 degrees is the same as 360 degrees (a full circle puts you back at the beginning position). Thus something can be 55 degrees ahead or 55 degrees behind. The 55 degrees behind is the same as being 360 degrees minus 55 degrees, or 305 degrees.

Lost? You're not alone. There's a reason astrology got popular after computer programs were written to do the math. Prior to computers, astrologers would spend hours just doing the math for one chart. In fact, logarithms[1] were invented by an astrologer to make the math easier!

Let's look at some examples starting on the next page.

> David's chart is on the facing page. If Mercury is stationing at 23 degrees Sagittarius and the Sun is at 20 degrees Leo, then Mercury is trine

[1] Logarithms were developed in 1614 by Baron Napier of Marchiston.

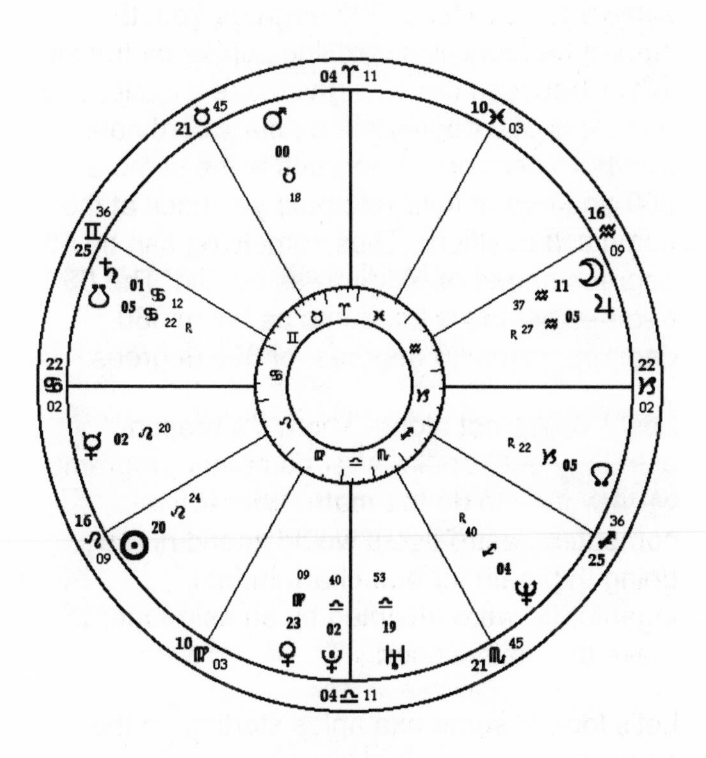

David's chart

the Sun by transit (see Appendix D to follow the math). If Mercury were anywhere from 10 degrees Sagittarius to 0 degrees Capricorn, it would be trine the Sun. Also, if Mercury were between 10 degrees Aries and 0 degrees Taurus, it would be trine the Sun.

So what does that mean? Each aspect has a general flavor, as listed in Table 5.

Table 5. What Do Aspects Mean?

Aspect	General Definition
Conjunction	The two planets may or may not get along. A balancing act is needed to meet the needs of both planets. The planets will bring out the best of each other or the worse. It may be difficult to separate out how the planets function because they are so intertwined.
Sextile	The two planets work well together. The energies are symbiotic, sibling like.
Square	The two planets get in each other's way; however, you can balance the energies by intentionally using the positive qualities of each.
Trine	The two planets highlight each other's good points. They are in harmony.
Opposition	The two planets are in an antagonistic role and will get in each other's way. They are, however, like two sides of the same coin, and so might complement each other if you allow them to do so.

Table 6 gives a short keywords list for the planets.

Table 6. Keywords for the Planets

Planet	Keywords
Sun	basic identity, life force, will, essence
Moon	emotion, security needs
Mercury	communication, transportation, thinking
Venus	relationship to people, places, things, art, music, beauty, valuables, romance
Mars	activity, aggression, assertiveness, power, sexuality
Jupiter	philosophy, religion, growth, expansion, prosperity, liberalism
Saturn	structure, limits, discipline, conservatism
Uranus	innovation, invention, rebellion
Neptune	the unconscious, mystical, intuition, illusion
Pluto	power, transformation, death, destruction, deep resources

By combining the keywords for two transiting planets with the general flavor of the transiting aspect, you know how to interpret the transiting aspect.

Continuing with David's chart as the example, if Mercury is trine the Sun, then this person's thinking may be especially clear (Mercury) about what is essential (Sun). As such, it is a good time to re-evaluate priorities and get the different elements of life in alignment.

In the next chapter, we'll put together the transiting houses and transiting aspects to determine how a specific Mercury retrograde interval might affect an individual. I'll also give you a table to help you quickly determine which planets are in aspect by transit to Mercury during the retrograde interval.

Putting It All Together

Let's put all of this information together by looking at a sample chart (see the next page). How did Mercury retrograde from February 21 to March 14, 2000 affect Susan?

Direction	*Date*	*Time*	*Location*
Retrograde	Feb 21 2000	12:40	17°Pi11'
Direct	Mar 14 2000	20:34	02°Pi48'

These are the steps for determining how a specific Mercury retrograde will aspect a chart. Notice that for the retrograde and shadow parts of the Mercury retrograde cycle, we do not pay any attention to aspect orbs outside of the path of the retrograde. In other words, if the retrograde path is from 13 Pisces to 2 Pisces, we ignore the 10 degrees before and after the outer edges of the retrograde path. This

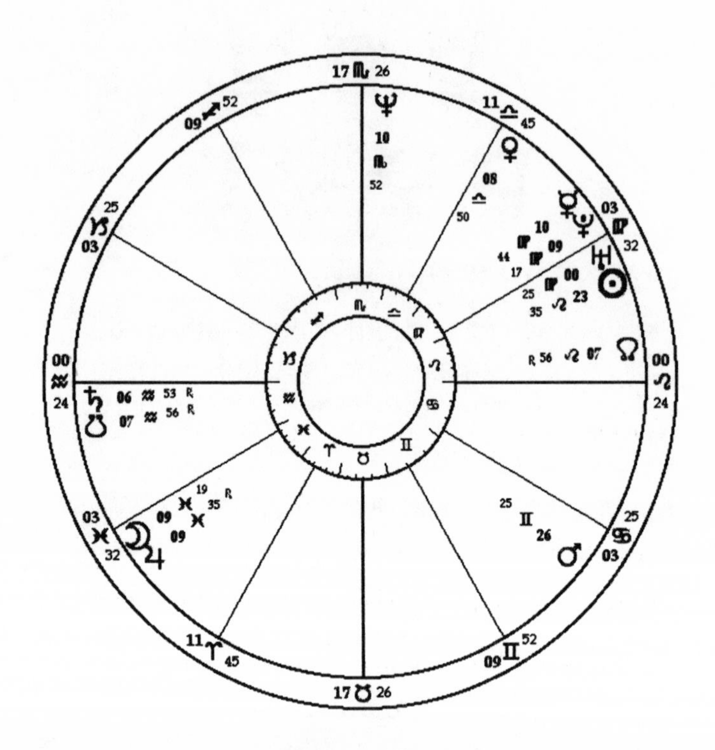

Susan's chart

actually makes it easier to determine which planets and houses are under the transit's influence. (However, do pay attention to the aspect orbs as soon as Mercury gets beyond its shadow.)

1. Where was transiting Mercury in the astrology chart?

> In this case, the whole retrograde period was in the second house. Therefore, Susan was expecting second house issues to be important, such as values, resources, talents, fears, and money.

2. Determine which planets were aspected by transit. To do so:

a) Check the degrees that Mercury was traveling through while retrograde (ignore the sign for now).

> In this case, 17 to 2.

b) Which signs might have been in aspect (ignore the astrology chart for the moment)? See Appendix F for quick look-up lists of which signs are in which aspect.

> Whenever Mercury is retrograde in Pisces, Mercury will be:
>
> - conjunct in Pisces
> - opposite in Virgo

- trine in Cancer and Scorpio
- square in Gemini and Sagittarius
- sextile in Taurus and Capricorn

c) Check the astrology chart for any planets in the indicated degrees and signs.

Table 7. Which Planets Are in Aspect During This Mercury Retrograde Period

Planet	Position	By Sign?	By Degree?	In Aspect?
Sun	23 Leo	no	no	not in aspect
Moon	9 Pisces	yes	yes	yes, conjunct
Mercury	10 Virgo	yes	yes	yes, opposite
Venus	8 Libra	no	yes	not in aspect
Mars	26 Gemini	yes	no	not in aspect
Jupiter	9 Pisces	yes	yes	yes, conjunct
Saturn	6 Aquarius	no	yes	not in aspect
Uranus	0 Virgo	yes	no	not in aspect
Neptune	10 Scorpio	yes	yes	yes, trine
Pluto	9 Virgo	yes	yes	yes, opposite

3. Using the keyword table for the planets (Table 6) combined with the keyword table for the aspects (Table 5), come up with a possible interpretation for the transiting aspect(s).

Mercury conjunct Moon (Pisces): Intense emotions may surface but be difficult to communicate

Mercury conjunct Jupiter (Pisces): Desire to expand knowledge and personal philosophy

Mercury opposite Pluto (Virgo): Tendency to over-criticize or to be extra sensitive to other people's words; words trigger deeply hidden memories

Mercury opposite natal Mercury (Virgo): Difficulty understanding someone's position or inability to sit and listen to others; trouble with daily activities

Mercury trine Neptune (Scorpio): Easy access to unconscious; time for intense dreams

4. Keep track of what really happened. What corresponded to your interpretation? What did you learn from the experience?

Susan reported to me that she spent most of the three-week interval at home alone because she felt ultra-sensitive to her surroundings. She found being with other people difficult. She had trouble finding words. Simple concepts were almost impossible to convey to co-workers.

She reported unexpected mood swings. She had intense dreams that she couldn't remember well.

> Susan read numerous science fiction books and several autobiographies by people practicing unconventional religions.
>
> She frequently forgot to eat. In general, many daily habits didn't happen. She examined her values around food, exercise, and health and discovered that she had more information on these subjects than she realized, but wasn't applying most of it.
>
> She also discovered several unconscious attitudes toward money and debt that she decided she was ready to move beyond.

You might ask, "what about the orbs listed in Table 4? Shouldn't we take those into account?"

No. The focus of Mercury retrograde is the area that Mercury is moving back over, so focus on the planets that are exactly aspected. Ignore the orbs during the retrograde. Of course, as soon as Mercury leaves its shadow, start paying attention to orbs again.

> In this example, ignore planets outside of the 2-17 degree range until Mercury returns to 17 degrees Pisces (that is, leaves its shadow).

Let's look at Susan's chart in relation to an upcoming retrograde interval and what she can plan on doing or not doing during that time for optimal use of the Mercury retrograde energy.

Direction	*Date*	*Time*	*Location*
Retrograde	Sep 14 2002	19:32	13°Li14'
Direct	Oct 6 2002	19:19	28°Vi20'

Let's follow the same procedures as before.

1. Where will transiting Mercury be in the astrology chart?

In this case, the retrograde will start in the 9th house and move back into the 8th house.

Susan can expect issues around philosophy, religions, travel abroad, and other cultures (9th house) to be on her mind, as well as death, transformation, power, and other people's resources (8th house) to be issues.

2. Determine which planets are aspected by transit. To do so:

a) Check the degrees that Mercury will travel through while retrograde (ignore the signs for now).

In this case, 13-0, 29, and 28.

b) Which signs might be in aspect (ignore the astrology chart for the moment)? See Appendix F for quick look-up lists of which signs are in which aspect.

Whenever Mercury is retrograde in Libra, Mercury will be:

- conjunct planets in Libra
- opposite planets in Aries
- trine planets in Aquarius and Gemini
- square planets in Capricorn and Cancer
- sextile planets in Sagittarius and Leo

But, since in this example Mercury moves from Libra back into Virgo, we need to look at potential Virgo aspects as well.

Whenever Mercury is retrograde in Virgo, Mercury will be:

- conjunct planets in Virgo
- opposite planets in Pisces
- trine planets in Taurus and Capricorn
- square planets in Gemini and Sagittarius
- sextile planets in Scorpio and Cancer

c) Check the astrology chart for any planets in the indicated degrees and signs.

Note: We need to do two charts because there are two signs involved. The first chart covers 13 degrees Libra to 0 degrees Libra. The second chart covers 30 degrees Virgo (which is the same as 0 degrees Libra) to 28 degrees Virgo.

Which Planets Are in Aspect During This Mercury Retrograde Period in Regards to 0-13 Degrees Libra

Planet	Position	By Sign?	By Degree?	In Aspect?
Sun	23 Leo	yes	no	not in aspect
Moon	9 Pisces	no	yes	not in aspect
Mercury	10 Virgo	no	yes	not in aspect
Venus	8 Libra	yes	yes	yes, conjunct
Mars	26 Gemini	yes	no	not in aspect
Jupiter	9 Pisces	no	yes	not in aspect
Saturn	6 Aquarius	yes	yes	yes, trine
Uranus	0 Virgo	no	yes	not in aspect
Neptune	10 Scorpio	no	yes	not in aspect
Pluto	9 Virgo	no	yes	not in aspect

Which Planets Are in Aspect During This Mercury Retrograde Period in Regards to 28-30 Degrees Virgo

Planet	Position	By Sign?	By Degree?	In Aspect?
Sun	23 Leo	no	no	not in aspect
Moon	9 Pisces	yes	no	not in aspect
Mercury	10 Virgo	yes	no	not in aspect
Venus	8 Libra	no	no	not in aspect
Mars	26 Gemini	yes	no	not in aspect
Jupiter	9 Pisces	yes	no	not in aspect
Saturn	6 Aquarius	no	no	not in aspect
Uranus	0 Virgo	yes	no	not in aspect
Neptune	10 Scorpio	yes	no	not in aspect
Pluto	9 Virgo	yes	no	not in aspect

Now take all the planets that are in aspect in at least one of the charts.

In this example, only two planets are under the retrograde influence.

- Mercury conjunct Venus
- Mercury trine Saturn

3. Using the keyword table for the planets (Table 6) combined with the keyword table for the aspects (Table 5), come up with a possible interpretation for the transiting aspect(s).

Mercury conjunct Venus (Libra) - Be prepared for unexpected communications (good or bad) from partners regarding the relationship; a good time for projects that combine aesthetics and the mind

Mercury trine Saturn (Aquarius) - Might feel the need to change daily habits or routines

4. To prepare for this Mercury retrograde time, Susan will want to arrange her activities to augment the energy of the retrograde and stay away from those activities likely to go astray.

Possible activities may be:

- Rearrange furniture (Mercury trine Saturn)
- Experiment with a new diet (Mercury trine Saturn)
- Encourage a partner to share something they've been reluctant to bring up (Mercury conjunct Venus)
- Read a mystery book (8th house)
- Watch travel videos (9th house) with a partner (Mercury conjunct Venus)

Make It Personal!

Generating a list of appropriate activities for yourself for a specific Mercury retrograde interval can be a rewarding activity. The following pages will help.

1. Copy your personal astrology chart onto the blank horoscope page. Appendix E lists the most commonly used glyphs so you'll be able to interpret the squiggles on your chart.

2. Fill in the stationing times and locations for the Mercury retrograde interval that interests you. See Appendix A for a list of station times and positions.

3. Go through each of the steps to generate a list of activities that will be appropriate for you during that interval.

4. Keep track of your experiences on the journal pages.

Many people find that after going through this procedure with their own astrology chart, everything makes more sense and is not as difficult as it first appeared. Give it a try.

My Astrology Chart

Name: ________________

Birth Date: _____________

Birth Time: _____________ a.m. p.m.

Birth Location: city ______________

state/province _________________

country _______________________

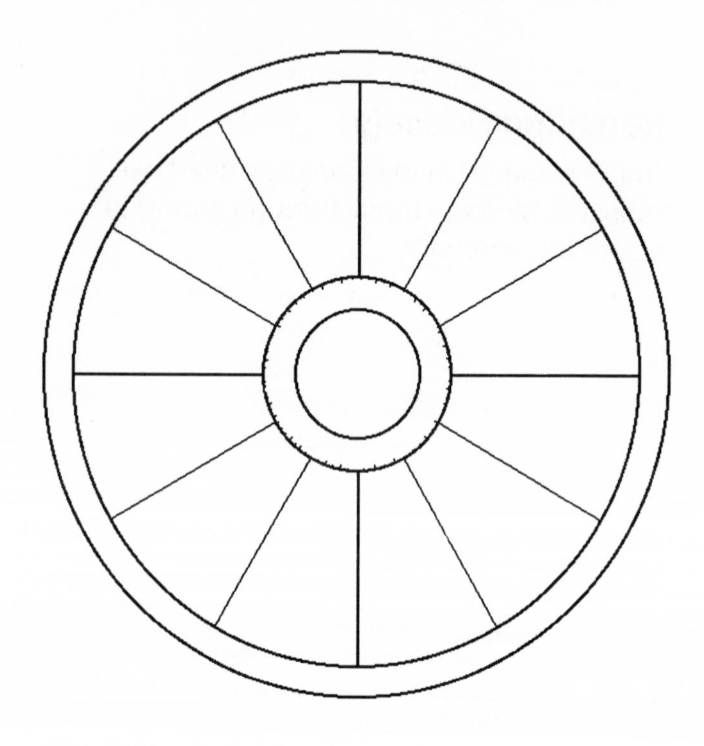

The Mercury Retrograde Interval That Interests Me

See Appendix A for the table data.

Direction	*Date*	*Time*	*Location*
Retrograde	___________	________	_________
Direct	___________	________	__________

Transiting House(s)

Which house(s) in my astrology chart will transiting Mercury travel through during this retrograde interval?

Transiting Aspect(s)

Determine which planets are aspected by transit. To do so:

1. Which degrees does Mercury travel through while retrograde (ignore the signs for now).

2. Which signs might be in aspect (ignore the astrology chart for the moment). See Appendix F for quick look-up lists of which signs are in which aspect.

Whenever Mercury is retrograde in ________ (fill in the sign), Mercury will be:

- conjunct in _________
- opposite in _________
- trine in ________ and __________
- square in ________ and __________
- sextile in ________ and __________

If Mercury is in two signs during the retrograde interval, do a table for each sign, as in the Chapter 10 example.

3. Fill in the potential aspects table. If Mercury retrograde travels in two signs during the interval, complete two tables, as in the example in Chapter 10.

Potential Aspects Table

Planet	Position	By Sign?	By Degree?	In Aspect?	Which Aspect?
Sun	_______	Y N	Y N	Y N	______
Moon	_______	Y N	Y N	Y N	______
Mercury	_______	Y N	Y N	Y N	______
Venus	_______	Y N	Y N	Y N	______
Mars	_______	Y N	Y N	Y N	______
Jupiter	_______	Y N	Y N	Y N	______
Saturn	_______	Y N	Y N	Y N	______
Uranus	_______	Y N	Y N	Y N	______
Neptune	_______	Y N	Y N	Y N	______
Pluto	_______	Y N	Y N	Y N	______

4. List all the planets that are in aspect.

a) Mercury is ______ (type of aspect) to _______ (planet)

b) Mercury is ______ (type of aspect) to _______ (planet)

c) Mercury is ______ (type of aspect) to _______ (planet)

5. Using the keyword table for the planets (Table 6) combined with the keyword table for the aspects (Table 5), come up with a possible interpretation for the transiting aspect(s).

a) ______________________________

____

b) ______________________________

____

c) ______________________________

____

6. Here is a list of activities that I want to do during this Mercury retrograde inteval:

- ______________________________
- ______________________________
- ______________________________
- ______________________________
- ______________________________
- ______________________________
- ______________________________
- ______________________________

Mercury Retrograde Journal

Write about your experiences during this Mercury retrograde interval. Include what happened and what you did. What do you want to do different during the next Mercury retrograde interval?

Keys to Thriving During Mercury Retrograde

More Stories

Many Mercury retrograde stories are funny, but only after the fact or if you're not involved. Here are some examples.

As If Missing Ballots Weren't Enough

> Just as Mercury went retrograde during February 2000, 4200 ballots for the Academy Awards were lost. Then, just before Mercury went direct that March, 55 of the statues were stolen from the loading dock. Most of them were found in a trash bin several blocks away after Mercury returned to direct.

Keep Your Mistresses Straight

A married guy was cheating on his wife with two mistresses who, in turn, didn't know about each other. That is, until one fateful day during a Mercury retrograde interval, when he sent each an e-mail message—but he sent the wrong messages to the wrong women. (From what I understand, his wife divorced him and the three women are now good friends.)

Do You Know Where Your Hands Have Been?

My friend agreed to work the late shift at a sandwich shop in a Florida college town during Mercury retrograde, despite there having been several robberies in the area over the past week. Just before closing, a man came in and ordered a sandwich. He opened the wax paper, took a bite, and then pulled out a gun and demanded all the money in the cash register. He left with the money and the sandwich, but left behind the wax paper with his finger prints.

Luggage Sees the World

The guy on the airplane told me about his last flight. He lived in Nicaragua and decided to fly up to California to visit relatives for a week. The plane met some bad weather on the way and was diverted to Phoenix. Several hours later, he boarded a different plane for Los Angeles. But his luggage didn't. Instead of getting on the plane to LA, his luggage was sent to Rio de Janeiro, then to Honolulu, and finally arrived in LA the day after he returned home to Nicaragua.

Which Restaurant?

Craig and I meet for lunch several times a month. One month, shortly after Mercury went retrograde, I called him and asked if he had time for a quick lunch at Peppers. He said yes, but asked that we meet at La Chosa because he was already downtown and needed to be on the north side of the city at 1:30. So off to La Chosa I went. After 1/2 hour, I called him on his cell phone. Turned out he was at Peppers wondering where I was.

"Time Stops For No Man"

My watch stopped working during Mercury retrograde, but I didn't have time to replace the battery. Good thing because as soon as Mercury went direct, the watch started working again.

One Ringy Dingy

A natural foods store replaced its existing phone system the day after Mercury went retrograde. The next day all 20 phones spread out over four floors started ringing at the same time and couldn't be stopped. The whole system had to be pulled out and reinstalled.

The Five Keys

These stories represent the five keys to surviving—make that thriving—during Mercury retrograde:

- Keep a sense of humor. Many Mercury retrograde stories have a funny side.
- Keep everything in perspective.
- Look for the golden egg. Mercury is telling you something: "slow down and smell the roses."
- "Engage brain before engaging mouth." (Or pressing SEND with e-mail.)
- Know that this too shall pass. Mercury will go direct, eventually. Life *will* return to "normal." Meanwhile, take this cosmic rest period seriously.

By adjusting your life-style to the cycles of the Universe, you can become friends with Mercury retrograde—and be well rewarded for your efforts.

Appendix A

Mercury Station Dates and Positions through December 31, 2014 at Greenwich, England

Direction	Date	Time	Location
Retrograde	Feb 21 2000	12:40	17°Pi11'
Direct	Mar 14 2000	20:34	02°Pi48'
Retrograde	Jun 23 2000	08:28	19°Cn57'
Direct	Jul 17 2000	13:16	10°Cn23'
Retrograde	Oct 18 2000	13:34	15°Sc48'
Direct	Nov 8 2000	02:21	29°Li58'
Retrograde	Feb 4 2001	01:51	00°Pi40'
Direct	Feb 25 2001	15:35	15°Aq25'
Retrograde	Jun 4 2001	05:16	29°Ge58'
Direct	Jun 28 2001	05:43	21°Ge17'
Retrograde	Oct 1 2001	19:17	29°Li41'
Direct	Oct 23 2001	00:16	14°Li14'

continued

Appendix A
continued

Direction	Date	Time	Location
Retrograde	Jan 18 2002	20:44	14°Aq28'
Direct	Feb 8 2002	17:22	28°Cp38'
Retrograde	May 15 2002	18:45	09°Ge59'
Direct	Jun 8 2002	15:07	01°Ge22'
Retrograde	Sep 14 2002	19:32	13°Li14'
Direct	Oct 6 2002	19:19	28°Vi20'
Retrograde	Jan 2 2003	18:12	28°Cp27'
Direct	Jan 23 2003	01:02	12°Cp19'
Retrograde	Apr 26 2003	11:54	20°Ta33'
Direct	May 20 2003	07:29	11°Ta08'
Retrograde	Aug 28 2003	13:36	26°Vi19'
Direct	Sep 20 2003	08:46	12°Vi13'
Retrograde	Dec 17 2003	15:54	12°Cp33'
Direct	Jan 6 2004	13:38	26°Sg17'
Retrograde	Apr 6 2004	20:22	01°Ta55'
Direct	Apr 30 2004	12:59	21°Ar07'
Retrograde	Aug 10 2004	00:27	08°Vi46'
Direct	Sep 2 2004	13:03	25°Le44'
Retrograde	Nov 30 2004	12:10	26°Sg45'
Direct	Dec 20 2004	06:22	10°Sg28'
Retrograde	Mar 20 2005	00:09	14°Ar05'
Direct	Apr 12 2005	07:40	01°Ar45'

continued

Mercury Station Dates and Positions

Appendix A
continued

Direction	Date	Time	Location
Retrograde	Jul 23 2005	02:55	20°Le28'
Direct	Aug 16 2005	03:45	08°Le46'
Retrograde	Nov 14 2005	05:36	10°Sg55'
Direct	Dec 4 2005	02:17	24°Sc46'
Retrograde	Mar 2 2006	20:23	26°Pi54'
Direct	Mar 25 2006	13:37	13°Pi11'
Retrograde	Jul 4 2006	19:28	01°Le22'
Direct	Jul 29 2006	00:33	21°Cn04'
Retrograde	Oct 28 2006	19:09	25°Sc04'
Direct	Nov 18 2006	00:18	09°Sc05'
Retrograde	Feb 14 2007	04:31	10°Pi13'
Direct	Mar 8 2007	04:38	25°Aq25'
Retrograde	Jun 15 2007	23:34	11°Cn35'
Direct	Jul 10 2007	02:10	02°Cn29'
Retrograde	Oct 12 2007	03:54	09°Sc04'
Direct	Nov 1 2007	22:52	23°Li23'
Retrograde	Jan 28 2008	20:25	23°Aq51'
Direct	Feb 19 2008	02:51	08°Aq20'
Retrograde	May 26 2008	15:43	21°Ge32'
Direct	Jun 19 2008	14:27	12°Ge59'
Retrograde	Sep 24 2008	07:11	22°Li50'
Direct	Oct 15 2008	19:59	07°Li35'

continued

Appendix A
continued

Direction	Date	Time	Location
Retrograde	Jan 11 2009	16:37	07°Aq45'
Direct	Feb 1 2009	07:04	21°Cp45'
Retrograde	May 7 2009	04:55	01°Ge44'
Direct	May 31 2009	01:16	22°Ta53'
Retrograde	Sep 7 2009	04:39	06°Li12'
Direct	Sep 29 2009	13:07	21°Vi37'
Retrograde	Dec 26 2009	14:31	21°Cp47'
Direct	Jan 15 2010	16:46	05°Cp34'
Retrograde	Apr 18 2010	04:01	12°Ta37'
Direct	May 11 2010	22:21	02°Ta40'
Retrograde	Aug 20 2010	19:53	19°Vi03'
Direct	Sep 12 2010	23:02	05°Vi23'
Retrograde	Dec 10 2010	11:58	05°Cp56'
Direct	Dec 30 2010	07:14	19°Sg38'
Retrograde	Mar 30 2011	20:42	24°Ar21'
Direct	Apr 23 2011	09:59	12°Ar53'
Retrograde	Aug 3 2011	03:46	01°Vi12'
Direct	Aug 26 2011	21:57	18°Le43'
Retrograde	Nov 24 2011	07:13	20°Sg06'
Direct	Dec 14 2011	01:36	03°Sg52'
Retrograde	Mar 12 2012	07:43	06°Ar49'
Direct	Apr 4 2012	10:05	23°Pi51'

continued

Appendix A
continued

Direction	Date	Time	Location
Retrograde	Jul 15 2012	02:10	12°Le32'
Direct	Aug 8 2012	05:34	01°Le26'
Retrograde	Nov 6 2012	22:58	04°Sg17'
Direct	Nov 26 2012	22:41	18°Sc12'
Retrograde	Feb 23 2013	09:35	19°Pi52'
Direct	Mar 17 2013	19:57	05°Pi39'
Retrograde	Jun 26 2013	13:03	23°Cn07'
Direct	Jul 20 2013	18:17	13°Cn22'
Retrograde	Oct 21 2013	10:22	18°Sc24'
Direct	Nov 10 2013	21:05	02°Sc31'
Retrograde	Feb 6 2014	21:37	03°Pi19'
Direct	Feb 28 2014	13:54	18°Aq10'
Retrograde	Jun 7 2014	11:51	03°Cn10'
Direct	Jul 1 2014	12:44	24°Ge23'
Retrograde	Oct 4 2014	16:56	02°Sc18'
Direct	Oct 25 2014	19:10	16°Li47'

Legend: Ar = Aries Ta = Taurus Ge = Gemini
Cn = Cancer Le = Leo Vi = Virgo Li = Libra
Sc = Scorpio Sg = Sagittarius Cp = Capricorn
Aq = Aquarius Pi = Pisces

Appendix B

Determining True Local Time of Stations

The Ballpark Figure

Sometimes you might like to know the approximate time that Mercury will station. You will need an ephemeris or astrological calendar.

Mercury stations at one time for the whole planet (you could call this cosmic time). Mercury stations at the same cosmic time in Beijing, China as it does in Sydney, Australia. But someone looking at her watch in Beijing will see a different time than someone looking at his watch in Sydney. Therefore, you must be aware of time zones to figure out what the time on your watch will say for the time of station.

When it's noon in London it is 7 a.m. in Washington, D.C. (Eastern Standard Time zone or EST) or 4 a.m. in San Francisco (Pacific Standard Time zone or PST). To ballpark figure the time of station, you need to know the time zone you are located in.

Most ephemera use Greenwich Mean Time (GMT) for all listed times. Adjust the listed time for your time zone by *subtracting* the number of hours for the time zone difference if you are west of Greenwich. For example, if Mercury stations at noon GMT, then it will be at 8 a.m. in Bermuda, 7 a.m. in New York City, 6 a.m. in Dallas, 5 a.m. in Denver, 4 a.m. in Los Angeles and 2 a.m. in Honolulu.

Should you be east of GMT, then add the time zone difference. At noon GMT, it is 1 p.m. in Paris and 5:30 p.m. in Calcutta. (Note: Many Asian and Middle Eastern countries have 1/2-hour adjustments, as well as hourly ones; Calcutta is one example. Check a time atlas or a professional astrology program.)

Be aware that, while most ephemeris use GMT, most astrological calendars use a local time zone. For example, Jim Maynard's calendars come with either Eastern or Pacific times listed (read the cover), while the Kickapoo Valley Garden Society's solarlunar calendar is based on Central Standard Time. Another difference is that ephemeris NEVER adjust for daylight savings time, wartime, or any other local adjustment. Most calendars do (the Kickapoo calendar is one of the rare ones that does not). So, for August 14, 1999, the calendar will list

Mercury stationing at 4:14 a.m. Eastern Daylight Time (EDT). You don't need to make any mathematical adjustments to use the calendar if you are in the time zone the calendar is based on (the makers of the calendar did the math for you!).

However, if you are using an ephemeris, you must take into account local time adjustments, such as daylight savings. So, to determine your clock time in Chicago on July 25, instead of subtracting 6 hours from GMT (C*S*T), you only subtract 5 hours (C*D*T).

Be careful, though, because local time adjustments are not consistent. For example, all of Indiana EXCEPT Indianapolis uses daylight savings time. So, on September 1, you would subtract 5 hours (CDT) from GMT if you were in Terre Haute, but subtract 6 hours (CST) if you were in Indianapolis.

Now for another snag. For astrological purposes, every 15 degrees longitude is another time zone. But in reality, governments don't use that precise adjustment for their clocks. So, although Biloxi is at 88W53 where you'd expect Eastern time zone, all of the state of Mississippi uses Central. So, for the purposes of ballpark adjustment, subtract 6 hours (Central) from GMT (or 5 hours during the summer). If you didn't know that Mississippi used Central time, you might instead subtract 5 hours (or 4 hours during the summer) and get the wrong local clock time. This is not a problem if you use the precise time method discussed next.

Precision Analysis

OK, Let's assume you have a project that you're working on and you need a drop-dead time to finish (before Mercury goes retrograde) or start (as Mercury goes direct). You want the exact time of station. The ephemeris or astrology calendar is going to give you a time, but it'll be a general time, either at GMT or for a specific time zone (such as Eastern).

As the world turns, approximately every 15 degrees longitude represents an hour. So, at 90 degrees west (Central Standard Time zone), time is 6 hours behind GMT (that's 90 degrees ÷ 15 degrees per hour). But very few cities are on the exact time zone line. A given city can be anywhere in the 15 degrees before the next time zone line.

Here's where True Local Time (TLT) comes in. Get the exact longitude of the city. Then follow the steps below:

1. Determine the local time zone used in that city. Find out if daylight savings or wartime was in effect for the date.

2. Determine number of degrees east/west of the astrological longitudinal line used in #1.

3. Multiply #2 by 4 minutes per degree

4. Add to #1 if west, subtract from #1 if east.

5. Add to GMT if east of Greenwich, subtract from GMT if west of Greenwich for the True Local Time (TLT).

6. Subtract one less hour if daylight savings or wartime was in effect.

(Notice that steps 4 and 5 are opposites in term of whether to add or substract if east or west.)

Let's take Minneapolis, Minnesota. An atlas tells us that the City of Lakes is located at 93W16 (93 degrees 16 seconds west of GMT). Minneapolis uses Central time, which starts (for astrological purposes) at 90 degrees west.

> 1. Central time is defined as 90 degrees west of Greenwich, which is 6 hours (90 degrees ÷ 15 degrees/hour)
>
> 2. Minneapolis is 3 degrees west of central time longitude (93 = 90 - 3)
>
> 3. 3 degrees x 4 minutes/degree = 12 minutes
>
> 4. West, so add 12 minutes to the 6 hours listed in #1

5. True local time is 6 hours 12 minutes less than GMT.
6. If daylight was in effect, then the true local time would be 5 hours 12 minutes less than GMT.

When Mercury stations at 12:52 GMT, it'll be 6 hours, 12 minutes less or 6:40 a.m. in Minneapolis. (If during the summer, it'll be 5 hours, 12 minutes less or 7:40 a.m. in Minneapolis.)

OK, what about Biloxi. You'll remember from the ballpark example that Biloxi should be Eastern time because of its longitudinal location but is actually within the Central time zone.

1. Central time is defined as 90 degrees west of Greenwich, which is 6 hours
2. Biloxi is 2 degrees east of the longitudinal line (88 - 90 = -2, we ignore the "-")
3. 2 degrees x 4 minutes/degree = 8 minutes
4. East, so subtract 8 minutes from 6 hours (#1)
5. True local time is 5 hours, 52 minutes less than (west) of GMT.

So, when Mercury stations at 12:52 GMT, it'll be 7:00 a.m. in Biloxi, Mississippi.

Now, what's great about TLT is that it is always TLT. Remember in the ballpark example, we could be an hour off if we thought Biloxi used Eastern time. Let's make that mistake.

1. Eastern time is defined at the 75 degrees west of Greenwich, which is 5 hours

2. Biloxi is 13 degrees west of the longitudinal line (88- 75 = 13)

3. 13 degrees x 4 minutes/degree = 52 minutes

4. West, so add 52 minutes to 5 hours (#1)

5. True Local Time in Biloxi is 5:52 less than (west) GMT. The same result as when we used the "correct" time of Central Standard. We can stand in city hall in Biloxi and the clock will read 7:00 a.m., whether we realize what time zone we are in or not.

True Local Time is True Local Time.

Appendix C

Are You The Exception (Born with Mercury Retrograde)?

If you have a retrograde Mercury in your natal chart, then you might be wondering what all the hoopla is about since to you what's happening is *normal*. Your whole life is about thinking things through before acting (or about learning to do so). My recommendation to you is to sit back and enjoy it as the remainder of the world visits your planet.

Retrograde Mercury natives don't think the same way as people born with Mercury direct. This can be a great asset! Retrograde Mercury natives naturally think "outside of the box." While this may seem to be a handicap when in positions that require you to follow the rules and toe the line (like during elementary school), it's a great asset in the work place—you are a natural problem solver. Choose jobs that allow you to show off your uncanny abilities to see through the problem and to devise solutions that others don't see until after you've shown them the new way to look at the situation.

Some retrograde Mercury natives notice that life gets much easier during Mercury retrograde intervals. Jobs may be offered to you, information that you need appears, and the contract goes through without the "normal" problems.

Generally speaking, you do not need to pay *special* attention when Mercury goes retrograde because you need to pay attention to Mercury *all* of the time.

Appendix D

Using Polar Coordinates to Determine Aspects

If you are doing your own mathematics, you'll have an easier time determining aspects if you convert the positions to polar coordinates. The table shows the conversions:

Degree to Polar Coordinate Degrees

0 degrees Aries	=	0 degrees
0 degrees Taurus	=	30 degrees
0 degrees Gemini	=	60 degrees
0 degrees Cancer	=	90 degrees
0 degrees Leo	=	120 degrees
0 degrees Virgo	=	150 degrees
0 degrees Libra	=	180 degrees
0 degrees Scorpio	=	210 degrees
0 degrees Sagittarius	=	240 degrees
0 degrees Capricorn	=	270 degrees
0 degrees Aquarius	=	300 degrees
0 degrees Pisces	=	330 degrees

So, 19 degrees Aries is 19 degrees in the polar coordinate system. (I warned you that there was math involved!)

> 9 degrees Sagittarius is 240 degrees (= 0 degrees Sagittarius) + 9 degrees = 249 degrees polar coordinates.
>
> 17 degrees Cancer is 90 degrees (= 0 degrees Cancer) + 17 degrees = 107 degrees polar coordinates.

Why go to all this bother? It makes aspects easy. Take the polar coordinates of each planet, subtract them, and then check to see if that difference is within the orb of one of the aspects.

For example, if Mercury is at 21 degrees Libra and Venus is at 11 degrees Scorpio, to determine if they are in aspect to each other:

1. Convert each planetary position to polar coordinates.

> Mercury is 180 degrees (= 0 degrees Libra) + 21 degrees = 201 degrees polar coordinates
>
> Venus is 210 degrees (= 0 degrees Scorpio) + 11 degrees = 221 degrees polar coordinates

2. Subtract the larger from the smaller.

> 221 - 201 = 20 degrees

3. Check the aspect with the orb table.

   20 degrees is not within any of the aspects listed

4. Therefore, this position of Mercury is not in aspect to this position of Venus.

Major Aspects

Degrees Apart	Aspect Name	Symbol (Glyph)	Orb
0	conjunct	☌	0-10 or 350-360 degrees
60	sextile	⚹	50-70 or 290-310 degrees
90	square	□	80-100 or 260-280 degrees
120	trine	△	110-130 or 230-250 degrees
180	opposite	☍	170-190 degrees

For another example, Jupiter is at 17 degrees Taurus and Uranus is 20 degrees Aquarius.

1. Convert each planetary position to polar coordinates.

   Jupiter is 30 degrees (= 0 degrees Taurus) + 17 degrees = 47 degrees polar coordinates

   Uranus is 300 degrees (= 0 degrees Aquarius) + 20 degrees = 320 degrees polar coordinates

2. Subtract the larger from the smaller.

   320 - 47 = 273 degrees

3. Check the aspect table.

   273 degrees is within the orb of a square.

4. Therefore, this position of Jupiter is square this position of Uranus.

Let's look at the transiting example used in Chapter 9. Mercury is stationed at 23 degrees Sagittarius and the Sun is at 20 degrees Leo.

1. Convert each planetary position to polar coordinates.

   Mercury is 240 degrees (= 0 degrees Sagittarius) + 23 degrees = 263 degrees polar coordinates

   Sun is 120 degrees (= 0 degrees Leo) + 20 degrees = 140 degrees polar coordinates

2. Subtract the larger from the smaller.

   263 - 140 = 123 degrees

3. Check the aspect table.

   123 degrees is within the orb of a trine.

4. Therefore, this position of the Sun is trine this position of Mercury.

Also, if Mercury was between 10 degrees Aries and 0 degrees Taurus, it would be trine the Sun at 20 degrees Leo.

1. Convert each planetary position to polar coordinates.

 Mercury is between 10 degrees polar coordinates (0 = 0 degrees Aries + 10) and 30 degrees polar coordinates (30 degrees = 0 Taurus)

 Sun is 120 (= 0 degrees Leo) + 20 degrees = 140 degrees polar coordinates

2. Subtract the larger from the smaller.

 140 - 10 = 130 degrees and 140 - 30 = 110 degrees

3. Check the aspect table.

 110-130 degrees defines the orb of a trine

4. Therefore, these positions of Mercury are trine the Sun, just as the previous example.

Aspects may be in either direction. When a transiting planet is approaching a natal planet's location, it is called "applying." When the transiting planet is past the natal planet's position, it is called "separating."

Appendix E

Glyphs

Glyph is a fancy word for symbol. Using glyphs, instead of writing out the name of the sign, planet, asteroid, aspect, or other astrology situation provides two important things:

1. Doing so takes less room, so many glyphs may be fit into an area that only has room for one or two words. Imagine how crowded a horoscope chart would look if words were used instead of glyphs.

2. Glyphs are not language dependent, so someone who speaks only Greek will understand the glyph in the same way that someone who speaks only Sanskrit, although they will have names for the glyphs within their own language.

For example, ♃ is called Jupiter in English but Guru in Sanskrit. Both the American and the Indian astrologer knows what the glyph means but might not be able to talk to each other because of a language barrier.

Here is a legend for the most commonly used astrology glyphs.

Signs

♈	Aries
♉	Taurus
♊	Gemini
♋	Cancer
♌	Leo
♍	Virgo
♎	Libra
♏	Scorpio
♐	Sagittarius
♑	Capricorn
♒	Aquarius
♓	Pisces

Planets

☉	Sun
☽	Moon
☿	Mercury
♀	Venus
♂	Mars
♃	Jupiter
♄	Saturn
♅	Uranus
♆	Neptune
♇	Pluto

Miscellaneous

℞	Retrograde
D	Direct
AS	Ascendant
MC	Midheaven
☊ ☋	Lunar Nodes (North and South)
⊗	Pars Fortuna

Chiron/Asteroids

⚷	Chiron
⚶	Vesta
⚵	Juno
⚳	Ceres
⚴	Pallas Athena

Aspects

☌	Conjunction
⚹	Sextile
△	Trine
□	Square
☍	Opposition
Q	Quintile
⚼	Sesquiquadrate
∠	Semisquare
⚻	Inconjunction/Quincunx

Appendix F

Quick Aspect Table

Use the following tables to quickly determine which signs are in aspect. Use this table to complete your personal retrograde table in Chapter 11.

Conjunct and Opposite

If Mercury is Retrograde In	Then the Conjunct Sign Is	Then the Opposite Sign Is
Aries	Aries	Libra
Taurus	Taurus	Scorpio
Gemini	Gemini	Sagittarius
Cancer	Cancer	Capricorn
Leo	Leo	Aquarius
Virgo	Virgo	Pisces
Libra	Libra	Aries
Scorpio	Scorpio	Taurus
Sagittarius	Sagittarius	Gemini
Capricorn	Capricorn	Cancer
Aquarius	Aquarius	Leo
Pisces	Pisces	Virgo

Trines

If Mercury is Retrograde In	Then the Trine Signs Are
Aries	Leo, Sagittarius
Taurus	Virgo, Capricorn
Gemini	Libra, Aquarius
Cancer	Scorpio, Pisces
Leo	Sagittarius, Aries
Virgo	Capricorn, Taurus
Libra	Aquarius, Gemini
Scorpio	Pisces, Cancer
Sagittarius	Aries, Leo
Capricorn	Taurus, Virgo
Aquarius	Gemini, Libra
Pisces	Cancer, Scorpio

Quick Aspect Table

Squares

If Mercury is Retrograde In	Then the Square Signs Are
Aries	Cancer, Capricorn
Taurus	Leo, Aquarius
Gemini	Virgo, Pisces
Cancer	Libra, Aries
Leo	Scorpio, Taurus
Virgo	Sagittarius, Gemini
Libra	Capricorn, Cancer
Scorpio	Aquarius, Leo
Sagittarius	Pisces, Virgo
Capricorn	Aries, Libra
Aquarius	Taurus, Scorpio
Pisces	Gemini, Capricorn

Sextile

If Mercury is Retrograde In	Then the Sextile Signs Are
Aries	Gemini, Aquarius
Taurus	Cancer, Pisces
Gemini	Leo, Aries
Cancer	Virgo, Taurus
Leo	Libra, Gemini
Virgo	Scorpio, Cancer
Libra	Sagittarius, Leo
Scorpio	Capricorn, Virgo
Sagittarius	Aquarius, Libra
Capricorn	Pisces, Scorpio
Aquarius	Aries, Sagittarius
Pisces	Taurus, Capricorn

Appendix G

50 Things to Do During a Mercury Retrograde

1

Renegotiate contracts (but sign after Mercury goes direct).

2

Research new business ideas (but start after Mercury goes direct).

3

Investigate stocks, mutual funds, and bonds (but buy after Mercury goes direct).

4

Relax at the beach or the ski resort (be sure to book the trip before Mercury goes retrograde).

5

Rename a company or pet.

6

Redesign a project.

7

Renew wedding vows.

8

Reconnect to family, friends, and clients that you've been out of touch with.

9

Have reunions and family picnics.

10

Write letters.

11

Take an excursion you've been putting off.

12

Recontact a potential client who hasn't responded.

13

Resubmit resume or job application.

14

Reread a classic.

15

Redo a repair that didn't get the job done.

16

Adjust the budget.

17

Touch up the paint on the house.

18

Redo anything that didn't get done right the first time.

19

Restart an exercise program or diet that you've dropped.

20

Retry it.

21

Daydream—big.

22

Write in a journal.

23

Investigate your family tree.

24

Watch VCR tapes with important people (like your children).

25

Play checkers or chess or ....

26

Play in the snow—make angels, snowmen, forts, and igloos.

27

Splash in a puddle/sing in the rain.

28

Make chocolate chip cookies (or any other favorite from your childhood).

29

Redistribute jobs/chores.

30

Reminisce about the old times.

31

Read or re-read a mystery novel.

32

Rewrite your novel.

33

Review your stock portfolio's performance (but don't buy or sell until after Mercury goes direct).

34

Retreat to a monastery for quiet reflection.

35

Write your cares in the sand and then watch the waves wash them away.

36

Spring clean (prep for a garage sale that will happen after Mercury goes direct).

37

Re-evaluate goals—both personal and business.

38

Investigate restructuring your business (but wait until Mercury goes direct to implement).

39

Update your business plan.

40

Amend your taxes.

41

Call people you haven't talked to in a long time.

42

Re-enter data that's been lost.

43

Renew magazine subscriptions.

44

Re-organize the closets.

45

(re) Quit smoking/drinking.

46

Rearrange furniture.

47

Debate and examine all the options (but don't implement anything until Mercury goes direct).

48

Party (if formal, send invitations before Mercury goes retrograde; if casual, just call people a few hours before you want to start).

49

Follow-up on projects.

50

Do regression or hypnotherapy work.

Epilogue

Several people have asked me to write a short epilogue about the story of this book. Just as Heather Rowntree has observed, writing about any aspect of astrology manifests that aspect in one's life. Seriously manifests that aspect.

For example, this book was suppose to go to press in April 1999. Now, a year later, with drastic changes to the organization and text, it's finally seeing its day at the offset press. I believe this version is a big improvement over the original; it's been worth the time needed to add more examples and more basic astrology.

Most of the revisions to this text have been during Mercury retrograde intervals. For one reason or another, I would not have time to work on it or the editor wasn't available when Mercury was direct. The only Mercury direct parts were the original draft, the artist's additions, and the current layout. (Well, actually the original layout was done during a Mercury retrograde and here I am, re-doing the design!)

I have endeavored to make this text reader-friendly without a lot of jargon or math. (Yes, there could have been more math.)

If you need to contact me with questions, please send them to my publisher. Include a self-addressed, stamped envelope and your astrology chart.

Therese Francis
c/o Crossquarter Breeze
PO Box 8756
Santa Fe, NM 87504-8756

I'm available for workshops, radio interviews, and book signings.

Crossquarter Breeze will print astrology charts for $5 (postage paid) if you send a check along with your name, birth date, birth time (include a.m. or p.m.) and birth location. If you don't know your birth time, at least provide an approximation (for example, "Mom says I was a lunch baby"). A phone number in case of questions is a good idea (especially if you send the order during a Mercury retrograde interval).

Here's to your new relationship with Mercury retrograde!

Gods & Goddesses of the Zodiac

A Coloring Book by Anne Marie Garrison

This delightful coloring book is a compilation of Anne Marie Garrison's sketches for Llewellyn's *1997 Astrological Calendar*. The cover is a full-color piece from Llewellyn's *1995 Astrological Calendar*.

The deities were chosen from Babylonian, Greek, Middle Eastern, Egyptian, Teutonic, Yoruba and Syrian pantheons.

Each of the 13 black & white, 6" x 9" sketches is on a separate page to prevent marker bleed through from damaging the next sketch. Below each sketch are keywords about the astrological sign. The facing page contains a description of the deity.

Gods & Goddesses of the Zodiac is a must for anyone interested in mythology or astrology.

ISBN: 1-890109-31-2 Cost: $6.95

Learn Astrology While Having Fun

Age of Aquarius Astrology

A Learning Game and Divination System

Age of Aquarius Astrology: A Learning Game & Divination System is four things in one:

- a way to learn astrology for individuals and groups
- a game for up to 6 people or teams
- a focus for group discussion
- a divination system

☍ This is a fun, flexible way to learn the language of astrology. This deck deals with general information on Western astrology, the 12 signs, the 12 houses and the 10 major planets and lights.

Age of Aquarius Astrology comes with:

- 78-card playing deck
- 6 marble playing pieces ♄
- 1 six-sided die
- 1 canvas playing board
- 1 instruction book/guidebook
- 1 canvas carrying case

ISBN: 1-890109-16-9 Cost: $29.95

The Mercury Retrograde Book

Surviving--Nay, Thriving--During Mercury Retrograde

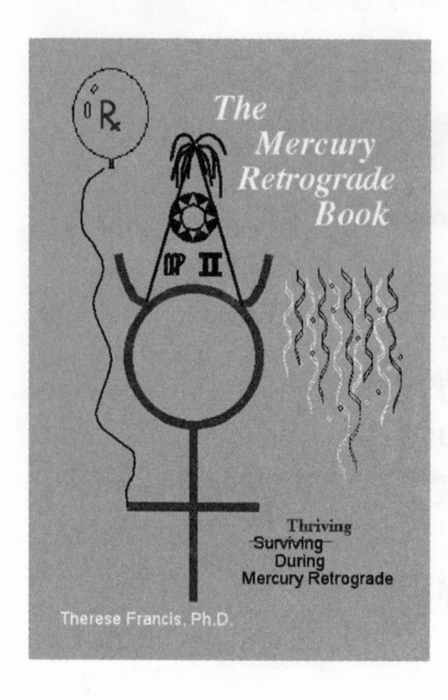

by Therese Francis

Change your view of these three-week intervals from enemy to friend by knowing what to do when. This book contains hundreds of ideas for you to do during the next Mercury retrograde interval that will improve, calm, and clarify your life.

ISBN: 1-890109-33-9 Cost: $12.95

Herb Pillows based on Natal Moon Signs

Special blends of herbs and spices specific for each lunar native to calm the mind, help with meditation, and improve sleep. Outer case is washable. Size is approximately 4" x 8" ("neck pillow size").

Cost: $18, send birth date, time and place with order

20 Herbs to Take Outdoors

An Herbal First Aid Primer for the Outdoor Enthusiast

by Therese Francis

According to a survey published in a recent Journal of the American Medical Association, one of the fastest growing areas of health care is the use of herbs. This easy-to-use herb book gets you and your family started with 20 easy-to-find herbal products.

- **Selected as outstanding by Parent Council®**
- **Selected by One Spirit Book Club** (a division of Book-of-the-Month Club)

Easy-to-follow instructions on finding the 20 products and using them for a variety of common injuries and illnesses that may occur when outdoors; no prior knowledge of herbs needed; no need to find the herbs on the ground (or take the chance of picking a dangerous look-a-like)

Convenient 4-1/4" x 5-1/2" size

ISBN: 1-890109-00-2 Cost: $6.95

To Order Products

Send payment and a photocopy of this order form to:
Crossquarter Breeze
PO Box 8756
Santa Fe NM 87504-8756

or fax your order to: (505) 438-9846

Qty	Description	Unit Price*
___	The Mercury Retrograde Book	$12.95
___	Gods & Goddesses of the Zodiac	$6.95
___	20 Herbs to Take Outdoors	$6.95
___	Age of Aquarius Astrology game	$29.95
___	LunaHerbal pillow	$18.00

First Name ______________ Birth Date ____________
Birth Time _____am pm Birth Location __________

Name: ____

Address: ______________________________________

City: ______________ State: _____ Zip: _________

PAYMENT METHOD

___ Check or money order
___ Credit card: ___ VISA ___ Mastercard ___ AmX

Name (if different on card) _____________________

Card Number __________________ Exp Date ____

Signature ____________________________________

*Please add shipping/handling and sales tax as follows:

Shipping & Handling: $1.95 for first item, $0.75 for each additional item to same address

New Mexican residents add 6.5% gross receipts tax to full order (including shipping)

Please allow 4-6 weeks for delivery.